TEST
YOUR
TRUTH

Your Call To Action!

MICHAEL L. USHER

The Usher Agency

**TEST
YOUR
TRUTH**

THE
USHER
AGENCY.

TO: ____

FROM: ____

Many of us move through the world unaware of how we show up in our communities. We act out of impulse instead of purpose.

Whether you are aware of it or not, Your truth is representing you every day. It is at the very core of all your intentions, your decisions and indecisions, your motivations, and ultimately your drive in life.

It shows up as the many voices in your head that are either working for you or against you. It shows up in your relationships where you either feel seen and valued for your true nature, or for your representative. It shows up in your place of work where your work either reflects your true purpose and is consistent with your life's mission, or not.

Your truth is fundamentally all that has shaped you to be who you are today.

TEST YOUR TRUTH Is Your Call To Action!

Comprised of 25 Truth Actions written from personal experience, in a poetic style; To inspire you to creatively dream bigger and bolder for yourself. And to start today to test your self, your love, your power, your relationships, and your ventures; With the ultimate goal of guiding and encouraging you to get closer to standing in your truth.

After every Truth, You are encouraged to personalize each one with an action you've either taken or will take by simply starting with I...

When you're done, Give yourself a truth score from 1 to 10 to see how close you are to that truth.

CONTENTS

| 1 |

WITH I STAND

Stand alone

in crowded rooms

with your head held high

and watch

as they pass you by.

There's some laughter

and blank stares in their eyes.

Ready to accept the challenge,

Walk up slowly with a calm

and greet them all with a smile.

Place a visual representation of your truth action here:

**Now think of how you can personalize this
truth into an action you've either taken or will take
by simply starting with I...**

YOUR TRUTH SCORE

1   2   3   4   5   6   7   8   9   10

| 2 |

REACH FOR THE MOON

Have a crazy dream

to reach for the moon.

Avoid words

like tomorrow,

next time,

or see you soon.

No matter where it takes you,

if you ever make it that far,

At least you'll land among the stars.

Place a visual representation of your truth action here:

Now think of how you can personalize this
truth into an action you've either taken or will take
by simply starting with I...

YOUR TRUTH SCORE

1   2   3   4   5   6   7   8   9   10

| 3 |

YOU ARE MORE

It's ok to feel

different from the rest.

In a world

where you don't have the luxury

to be second best.

Occupy every space

where you are outnumbered,

underestimated

and put to the test.

Place a visual representation of your truth action here:

**Now think of how you can personalize this
truth into an action you've either taken or will take
by simply starting with I...**

YOUR TRUTH SCORE

1   2   3   4   5   6   7   8   9   10

| 4 |

BORN TO CREATE

Always choose

the path less traveled by.

While others go right, go left.

With every rise and fall

let your teacher

become your experience,

And when they all see their fate,

you see an opportunity to create.

Place a visual representation of your truth action here:

Now think of how you can personalize this
truth into an action you've either taken or will take
by simply starting with I...

YOUR TRUTH SCORE

1   2   3   4   5   6   7   8   9   10

| 5 |

THE CRACKS

The magic of everything

exists in the cracks.

Whether fully developed

or never seen;

And placed beautifully

in between

all your perfect

and imperfect dreams.

Place a visual representation of your truth action here:

**Now think of how you can personalize this
truth into an action you've either taken or will take
by simply starting with I...**

YOUR TRUTH SCORE

1   2   3   4   5   6   7   8   9   10

| 6 |

HIS STORY

When you learn something new,

first ask yourself

who benefits

from it's truth or untruth.

Then research its origin

after being past down

from generation to generation,

And wonder why

this story

became history.

Place a visual representation of your truth action here:

**Now think of how you can personalize this
truth into an action you've either taken or will take
by simply starting with I...**

YOUR TRUTH SCORE

1   2   3   4   5   6   7   8   9   10

| 7 |

DOOR OPEN

Every time

you come close

to walking through.

Tell yourself

the door never existed,

the lock was already open,

and that the key

always belonged to you.

Place a visual representation of your truth action here:

**Now think of how you can personalize this
truth into an action you've either taken or will take
by simply starting with I...**

YOUR TRUTH SCORE

1   2   3   4   5   6   7   8   9   10

| 8 |

YOUR WHY

Try to listen

to that voice

in disguise,

that gut feeling

deep inside.

It somehow already knows

who you really are

and who you try to hide;

And in time

will always lead you back to your why.

Place a visual representation of your truth action here:

**Now think of how you can personalize this
truth into an action you've either taken or will take
by simply starting with I...**

YOUR TRUTH SCORE

1   2   3   4   5   6   7   8   9   10

| 9 |

UNDER-PROMISE TO OVER-DELIVER

Aim to deliver

more than

what is expected of you.

Peace comes from

fulfilling expectations

while remaining free,

by controlling your promises

and choosing when

to deliver

only what they can see.

Place a visual representation of your truth action here:

Now think of how you can personalize this
truth into an action you've either taken or will take
by simply starting with I...

YOUR TRUTH SCORE

1   2   3   4   5   6   7   8   9   10

| 10 |

TILL YOU WIN

Pave a road

with good intentions.

Every twist and turn

life will test your direction and conviction.

Will you sell your soul

to get there faster?

And pay the ultimate price

and always wonder

what will come after.

Place a visual representation of your truth action here:

Now think of how you can personalize this
truth into an action you've either taken or will take
by simply starting with I...

YOUR TRUTH SCORE

1   2   3   4   5   6   7   8   9   10

| 11 |

NOTHING WASTED

Every piece of your puzzle

was earned from your struggle.

After every high

came another low

that always feels like blow,

After every low

the only choice you have

is to pick-up another piece

and turn it into gold.

Place a visual representation of your truth action here:

Now think of how you can personalize this
truth into an action you've either taken or will take
by simply starting with I...

YOUR TRUTH SCORE

1 2 3 4 5 6 7 8 9 10

| **12** |

JUST CREATE

From a vision in your head,

to a sketch

is how creation starts.

The first step is all it takes

to bring an idea

into the light

and out of the dark.

Give it a name

and set it free,

let it fly high and low

and land wherever it may be.

Place a visual representation of your truth action here:

Now think of how you can personalize this
truth into an action you've either taken or will take
by simply starting with I...

YOUR TRUTH SCORE

1   2   3   4   5   6   7   8   9   10

| 13 |

TRUST VIBES

Learn to trust that honest place

in between what seems right and wrong.

Those moments from peek to valley

that never seems to last long.

A smile so bright, and in a second it's gone.

That peaceful silence when all conversation stops

and you can hear a pin drop.

In between those spaces

lies our truth, and our fears;

Till another moment reappears.

Place a visual representation of your truth action here:

Now think of how you can personalize this
truth into an action you've either taken or will take
by simply starting with I...

YOUR TRUTH SCORE

1   2   3   4   5   6   7   8   9   10

| 14 |

HEART BE FREE

Feel the movement inside.

Of a purpose that isn't yet clear of free.

It speaks a language

you can't yet translate or see.

It can open many doors

and bring you to your knees.

Just let your heart fly

in a space where it can be all it can be,

So you can add to a puzzle

where you see a missing piece.

Place a visual representation of your truth action here:

**Now think of how you can personalize this
truth into an action you've either taken or will take
by simply starting with I...**

YOUR TRUTH SCORE

1   2   3   4   5   6   7   8   9   10

| 15 |

WE ARE MORE

More can only be defined as more,

Plus equals plus.

One win leads to another,

But how does that measure us?

The more you give, the more is taken.

The more you receive, the more you want.

Then you make a cut;

And the less you give, the less is given,

But no one wins from an over flowing pot

and many empty cups.

Place a visual representation of your truth action here:

Now think of how you can personalize this
truth into an action you've either taken or will take
by simply starting with I...

YOUR TRUTH SCORE

1   2   3   4   5   6   7   8   9   10

| 16 |

PREPARE FOR LUCK

Let doing the work

become your mantra.

Focus on every detail

without a wonder

of how long or how many years.

Calculate every move with precision

just in case today is your day,

While you carry on and prepare

to either meet the opportunity

or be guided in another way.

Place a visual representation of your truth action here:

**Now think of how you can personalize this
truth into an action you've either taken or will take
by simply starting with I...**

YOUR TRUTH SCORE

1   2   3   4   5   6   7   8   9   10

| 17 |

WHAT IF WE

Be lead by your curiosity.

The unknown of what could be.

When you come together

to create,

just ask yourselves

what if we,

what if we.

Place a visual representation of your truth action here:

Now think of how you can personalize this
truth into an action you've either taken or will take
by simply starting with I...

YOUR TRUTH SCORE

1   2   3   4   5   6   7   8   9   10

| 18 |

WE ARE LOVE

What you want,

i want too.

We build bridges that divide us

and call them our truth.

I say i am me,

you say you are you;

But when we get lost

and forget our identities,

We become me,

and we become you.

Place a visual representation of your truth action here:

**Now think of how you can personalize this
truth into an action you've either taken or will take
by simply starting with I...**

YOUR TRUTH SCORE

1   2   3   4   5   6   7   8   9   10

| 19 |

EVERYTHING FROM NOTHING

You have the power

to be connected to everything

or nothing at all.

You can use your fears

in battle

to fight your scars,

or understand

that the path that lays before you

was already won for you

by the greatest of them all.

Place a visual representation of your truth action here:

Now think of how you can personalize this
truth into an action you've either taken or will take
by simply starting with I...

YOUR TRUTH SCORE

1   2   3   4   5   6   7   8   9   10

| 20 |

FIRST STEP

Why is the first step the hardest to take?

To decide to go forward blindly

when everyone else needs proof

and think there is so much at stake.

There are few moments in life

when you get a sign

or see a clear window that's made just for you;

You have the choice

to continue to ask why,

or just go through.

Place a visual representation of your truth action here:

**Now think of how you can personalize this
truth into an action you've either taken or will take
by simply starting with I...**

YOUR TRUTH SCORE

1   2   3   4   5   6   7   8   9   10

| 21 |

CHANGE GAME

Be the first to play a game

where you don't know the rules.

With a hand assembled

by your scraps and your truth.

As you watch others inherit

the exception not the rule;

Play to win

and make way for those waiting in the wings.

Play to win

so that you would never be first again.

Place a visual representation of your truth action here:

**Now think of how you can personalize this
truth into an action you've either taken or will take
by simply starting with I...**

YOUR TRUTH SCORE

1   2   3   4   5   6   7   8   9   10

| 22 |

PEACE IS POWER

If power is peace, and peace is power

then what do they truly mean?

Choose to carve out a seat at tables that aren't built for you.

Define your role and become who you know you can be.

As you grow into the image of perfection and imperfection

simultaneously

in the eyes of those who just don't want to see,

Let your peace become a truth that's reserved for you

and only those who dare to see you be;

And with that power, choose to move through the world

as you set yourself free.

Place a visual representation of your truth action here:

Now think of how you can personalize this
truth into an action you've either taken or will take
by simply starting with I...

YOUR TRUTH SCORE

1   2   3   4   5   6   7   8   9   10

| 23 |

SENSE YOUR LIFE

Smell that familiar smell

without them being here.

Try to see what they don't want you to see.

Touch the glow of there warm embrace.

Hear the silence

between there thoughts, that empty space;

As you marvel with grace

at what they've prepared,

And lean in for a taste.

Place a visual representation of your truth action here:

**Now think of how you can personalize this
truth into an action you've either taken or will take
by simply starting with I...**

YOUR TRUTH SCORE

1 2 3 4 5 6 7 8 9 10

| 24 |

BE COMING

Arrive in your life

to meet your greatness every day.

Be your own comfort

to challenge what you and they have to say.

Dance in your position

and sing your name,

while you own

and become your lane.

Place a visual representation of your truth action here:

Now think of how you can personalize this
truth into an action you've either taken or will take
by simply starting with I...

YOUR TRUTH SCORE

1   2   3   4   5   6   7   8   9   10

| 25 |

YOU COULD

If what you have makes them feel less than,

then what is your true intention?

You've driven in the fast lane,

And dined among the one percent.

Dripped yourself in the very best

while you watch others envy at your flex.

It isn't a challenge anymore, to let your ego be the cure

when you're misunderstood.

So just let your greatest flex,

be that you could.

Place a visual representation of your truth action here:

Now think of how you can personalize this
truth into an action you've either taken or will take
by simply starting with I...

YOUR TRUTH SCORE

1   2   3   4   5   6   7   8   9   10

You are now one step closer to standing
with power in your truth.

If this book inspired you, Please share the message with someone you want to inspire.

Their Names:

____

____

____

Thank You for taking the time.

theusheragency.com